I0200300

**Sustainability.**

art, poetry, tea and roses.

# rosewater

DIAMOND MATHIEU

Soursop Media
Copyright © 2021 Diamond Mathieu


All rights reserved. No parts of this book may be
reproduced in any form, including electronic, recording,
photography, or otherwise, without the written
permission of the publisher or author.

Rosewater
ISBN-13: 978-0692876084
ISBN-10: 0692876081

rosewater- (n) water infused with rose petals, used as perfume and for culinary purposes, as well as, in medicinal preparations.

(n) the byproduct of roses. A personification of the remnants of the worst storm, that somehow becomes the origin of beautiful, organic, true art.

I finally found my purpose;
its writing.
I was born to write,
I know this now.
I was born to create in general,
to produce art,
to love and feel deeply.
But above all,
I was put here to write.

## Rose bush; house by the beach

Nothing will be sweeter than the rebirth of my garden.
It's the only thing
that keeps me smiling these days.
It's what keeps me going.
I am ready to experience the more tender and fruitful
side to life.
The worst is behind me.
I am open to all pure and positive things that are meant
for me.
Throughout this healing journey,
I will create and give continuously.
I will reclaim my identity.

I could've painted a picture one million times of what
the past three years has been like, but I still don't think
you could've felt the entirety of my emotions unless you
existed with me in every moment; in every scene. It was
paining up until a point that I no longer felt. I became
numb. Still on some days, I was met with enough
emotion to paint a sky with. I became half of myself, and
somehow, I found the strength to rebuild myself with
words.
I rebuilt my body with words.

Thank God for this new chapter.

There is no time like the present.
I feel as if I'm overflowing
with an ocean-sized amount of
peace, love and understanding,
because I shamelessly chose
to dedicate myself to my purpose
and to follow my destiny.
What a blessing; I'm so grateful.

Sometimes the soul requires a bit of security so I
began to write myself a home of my own;
in my own mind.
Where have I been, you ask?
I've been constructing poetry and
I am ready to share them now.

As a result of fear,
I spent the elapse of three weighted years
folding my tongue in half,
as to stop *beautiful, beautiful* language
from forming
from its muscle.

But adversity cannot stop the poet,
because even when words
do not flow from the mouth like a river,
they are still standing firm in the mind.
Here is my tryptic.
A literary representation of my healing journey.

## Think about it, then answer. (For me, its words)

Not whom,
but what are you married to?
What holds onto your hand faithfully in union and
never lets go?
What is in your corner
no matter how many times
you are left spinning in circles?
When both mind and body mimics the
spiral of exiled petals,
what is it that bowls its hands together
in a concave embrace to catch you?
And lastly, what makes you better?

## Rain before the rebirth

It shall rain rose petals tonight;
a moment after the sky
has closed its eyes for slumber and
the moon has arrived once again
to listen to hopeful hearts.
I will dance until the magnitude of
floral blessings underneath my feet rises up
and unites with the rainfall
and becomes rosewater.
A zephyr of petals will cascade onto my skin,
like delicate kisses from a lover.
Thousands of rose petals raining down on me
because the clouds are overcome with love.
These sorts of things are not peculiar.
Believe me,
they have happened for me
a million times over;
in my wildest dreams.
I have been telling others my entire life
that the rain
can take on the form
of roses.

## First name

The way you say my name
breathes new life into the
soul of the two-syllable word
that was chosen
as a title for others to use,
to grab my attention
when I am dancing in my imagination.
Each letter that leaves your tongue
in an act of pronunciation
makes my heart run warm.

My epithet;
like the precious stone of everlasting love.
A brilliant, that sparkles with
the most delicate touch of light,
known to be
one of the toughest substances
discovered upon Earth.
Indestructible;
you couldn't tell by its sheer beauty.
Before this,
I don't think I have ever
gotten used to others
calling out to me
like a form of crystal that is said
to last a lifetime;
like those pressured rocks
that refuse to break.
**DIAMOND.**
But why is it when you say my name,
am I left serenaded in jewels of my namesake?
I am left feeling royal.

When you call me:
*Adamas. Diamanté. Almasi. Dyaman. Lu'u-Lu'u.*
*Je suis fou de toi.*

*Je t'aime.*
Your voice makes the stars fall onto us
and they bury themselves
in the ground to be born again.
CALL THEM DIAMONDS.

You've made them pure and of raw crystal.
A voice that makes free formed things solid rock.
The way you place my name on my eardrums,
it's like placing baguettes along my fingers.
I'm married to your sound.
I'm adorned in your words.
You say it like you
jotted it down in your journal
and chose it specifically for me,
like you have witnessed hidden facets
within me that I have yet to see.
When I'm stuck in a daydream,
you often whisper sensually into my ear that
you see my name as befitting,
and as the sunlight tumbles onto me,
somehow I begin to glisten from all the blushing.

In the skies,
above our loving minds,
they share an array of divine fruit,
as they bestow a blessing of rainfall upon us,
creating a perfect moment,
and you embrace the raindrops as they join our skin.
Mid-celebration, you scream "DIAMONDS!"
as if the precipitation was a plentitude
of beautiful, jeweled mineral substance.
By now our bodies are painted in rain
and has begun to draw in water and love, like sponge.
You murmur my name and
I draw nearer to your frame;
fitting myself neatly into the outlines of your physique,
like collage-making.

But is there even so much enchantment
spoken in a name?
The way you utter my name
makes dust and dandelions raise up
and cover those seven letters in an act of protection.
How very selfish would it be
to presume that title be reserved
just for me,
all because you croon my name
like it left raw honey
on the tip of your tongue,
so when you call out to me I am left bewildered;
lost looking for the orchestra
that plays alongside you.
Are you trying to get me to look your way,
or are you digging into the earth
to find precious stones?
Which one is it?
Your voice echoes
in ripples of emotion,
*from the skies,*
*to the warmth of jewel mines.*

I constantly ask myself,
who reigns supreme
when it comes to unlocking the gates
of my everlasting love?
The answer was already spoken for me.
Call on me.
But is there even so much enchantment
spoken in a name?

## *Yeux marrons*

I remember the way
the light burst through the windows
and hit your eyes, like they were painted glass.
*In hues of deep brown and muted gold painted in the*
*foreground.*
Copper. Molasses. Both copper and molasses.
*Browning* caramelizing in a wedding pot,
clay, the color of cacao being formed in the hand
of an artist,
nutmeg, cinnamon and anise.
*(Your stare outshines all of these.)*
And never have I witnessed
eyes that left me
so moved
that I could cry.

I found myself trying
to decipher the emotion
and meaning within
the mosaic tile of your stare;
as if you were fine art.
And I said to myself,
you belong in the museum,
or maybe even in my arms.
I'm a lover of the arts
and of beautiful souls,
and I would appreciate you as both.

(Your eyes and beautiful skin tone both originate from
the same shade of brown.
How unique, how deep, how moving and inspirational.
I often steal glances at you while you are submerged in
your life work. I love you♥)

## Rose union

You'll know when love finds you.

You'll be busy tending to your garden,
speaking sweetly to the flowers and
clipping away withered ends,
with your two knees
buried in the rich and fertile dirt.
That is when you'll feel a reminiscent joy
fill your vessel
and a smile form inside of you.
From deep inside you.
A warmth you've longed for.
And that feeling has a face,
it has a name:
*Your Lover,*
has tiptoed gracefully into your mind.
Internalize the daydream
so that it fills up your heart to the brim.
Don't let that feeling leave you, love is yours to keep.

You're in love.
(Let love carry you like heaven's raindrops placed in the
belly of a weightless cloud.)

You're in love.
(Love is like a second sun. Through it all things obtain
the energy to thrive.)

You're in love.
(Isn't it beautiful?)

Love begins in the garden.

## Emotional Precipitation

I have fallen for you,
it's in my nature to.
Ask the ripened fruit,
the tears of sulking clouds,
and the fainting leaves
how it feels.

All of me,
scattered in pieces.
A beating heart and a colorful soul,
loving for all to see.
And it feels so good,
as you catch the very best parts of me
in your hands.

## Day-clean

When you get dressed this morning,
you should put on my love.
Before your cologne,
let love overfill this room
like clouds unbounded.
Some days I look at you
and wonder if the right words
exist on the human tongue to
describe admiration for another.
If you are also overcome with passion this morning,
guide my hand to the place where
your heart rents a room,
(a cozy little lover's studio within your temple)
so that I can witness the emotional waves
flowing through you,
that makes you an ocean in your own right.
Show me where your affection
rises and sets
each loving day.
At dawn and at eventide,
I often talk to the sky about you.

Before you put on your watch,
let me tell you of all the *times* I've fallen for you,
again
and again.
Words lend intimacy sometimes.

Before you drape your coat over
the crescent of your shoulders,
kiss my lips with the romance
of a room full of roses.
Layers of cloth could never
keep me as warm as your love.
If ever there are days
that you have wondered

if you were more or less like the sun,
never doubt your purpose.
My dear,
worry less and shine more.
If only you knew
how you bring an abundance of light
to those living amongst you,
you would be left in amazement.
Your smile would never
leave your face for a second.
I hope you know
that when you speak,
people stop to listen.
I hope you know
that your ideas and your feelings
are of the utmost importance.
I could go on and on
about the many reasons why I love you.
There would be
letters upon letters
celebrating your name.

You deserve the very best love there is.
You are special.
I tell you that often and
sometimes you smile,
then blush and look away,
but I don't know if you hear me though.
I have no problem repeating myself:
**You are special,**
beyond words,
beyond words could ever convey.

Before you lace up your shoes
and turn to face the world,
let me wrap you in my embrace,
like the most delicate ribbon
on a precious gift,
because that you are.

You're loved.

## Pursue

Are you sure this is what you want?
Some things are life-changing,
but if it's bliss you desire,
*get to know me.*
My allure will dance circles around you
and make you think
this world were mine.
Let me bring my love to you,
like an enticing pecan pie crafted by loving hands;
sweet, tender, and warm.
Watch it come your way,
like a glistening, chrome metro train
that has your attention
wrapped up in a daze (speeding past you)
and if you hesitate, you'll miss your only chance.
Don't take me lightly.
Don't take me lightly.
**Don't take me lightly.**
This is the magic you dream of,
standing before you in the physical.
My love would be something
you would never want to end.
**But good things are everlasting.**

## Roses were the first flowers in existence

Do roses know that they are roses?
Do they know that they are beautiful?
Do roses need to be aware that they are roses
in order to grow?

I have asked myself these questions
forty-three times,
amidst my daydreams,
as I step out of the shower
and rub rose oil onto my skin,
as well as,
during the hours that I usually paint in silence,
and the answer has yet to reveal itself to me.
But they grow anyway,
and **my** are they are beautiful!
Don't you agree?

But if a rose awakes at dawn,
and the sun strikes its first ray
from that rose into the river
and a reflection is produced,
and that rose's mirrored likeness is noticed
from the deep corners of its eyes and
that rose realizes it is a rose,
beauty and grace will merge and produce power.
We will learn to appreciate roses in a new way.
But maybe roses already know that they are roses,
because they seem to hold their heads upright
with such dignity.

Do roses beam with elation and blush humbly
whenever praises of their regality
are tucked in between conversation?
And how lovely are roses?

I once visited a garden
on the way to *Palatuvier,*
and out of all the flowers
living in the garden,
the roses that shined beet-red
were the ones I favored most.

**In love; not leaving (3:45 pm)**

In your eyes,
let's face it,
I am lost.
Too far gone.
I might as well call you home.

And after we share a kiss signifying trust and new
beginnings, you ask me to build with you.
May God bless this moment grounded in organic love.

*(You have my heart, love.*
*Please don't break it...praying you don't break it...)*

## The coffee shop on the beach

And just who do you think you are?
*(with your charming smile and your piercing stare.)*
Strands of light are reflecting softly off your skin
and the music playing is a description of you.
A master of hearts; you break into a reminiscence of
all the points of Earth where your tongue
has tasted the most delectable foods
created by the careful hands of mankind,
and my spirit is at peace to see
another so in love with life.
I look into your eyes
and say to you "summer"
and you respond "North Carolina".
In return you ask my favorite attribute of nature,
and in a tranquil tone,
I tell you that I would choose the ocean without a doubt.
It is 6:30 *post meridiem* and honestly,
I can feel myself falling for you.
The evening sun has *never*
descended before my eyes this way and I
cannot turn away from the sky
while it is painting a masterpiece.
The sky may have been inspired by you.

The tea here is wonderful
and so is telling the truth.
So as we sip on a brew of black tea and rose petals,
I mention to you that your energy is
like the waking of the sun; early dawn
and that your voice plays notes onto my heart,
like that of a skilled pianist.
You; a being blessed with a mind
as dimensional as a diamond,
but as free as our atmosphere.
I am amazed by you.

Don't think I haven't noticed
how you've lowered the clouds
and poured warm rain
into your palms as if it were nothing.
I've seen you grow flowers
with the slight touch of your fingertips;
how you nonchalantly
call on the birds to sing for me.
(I am enamored)
But I'm most blown away
by how you placed the sunset in your eyes.
When you look to me,
I can feel the sun dipping
and the intense colors flowing through my being.
I have fallen
for you the way rain does
on cold, stormy nights; hard and recklessly.
Something you're already privy to
because every emotion that enters my blood
is reflected in my stare.
I'm at my most vulnerable state when I'm with you.

So again,
I ask the question:
with your deep, smoky, vocal tone
and your persuasive speech,
just who do you think you are?

## In solitude, but never lonely

When my future lover
takes me by the hand
as to remind me of their love,
their love
for a healing soul like I,
I'll have no choice but to remember
that these very hands
wiped my own tears on sorrowful days
and carried agony unbelievable to the ears
and sadly,
I began to believe that's what they were made for;
to cater to pain.

This time around,
when my lover looks me in the eyes
and kisses my hand,
as to transfer love of a lifetime,
I may cry,
but this time only a few teardrops
that stream from the hidden corner of my eyes,
as to initiate change
and emanate joy.

(Heartbreak is a detrimental life lesson, but those very
lessons are imperative to growth. It really does get
better. All things in life must heal after affliction to
become a more resilient version of itself. After the *pain*,
you *persevere* and with time you will *prosper*, in all that
you do.  Take time to invest in your spirit. Love does not
need to be hunted down, but instead it will find you.
Just like your calling, and your truth, love will find you.)

# I promise I'll mail this love letter off in the morning

Adonis,
being able to converse fluently
in love language with you,
enlivens me.

Inamorato,
My love for you has become a beach,
with devoted waves that always
return home to shore
in an infinite cycle.

Honey,
you deserve the world
and a collection of all the things
that leave you bursting with joy,
left in a bundle on your doorstep
in the early of a brisk, autumn day.

My love, my love,
I am here
dancing sensually in my emotions
and creating watercolor pigment
with cheerful tears and what is left
of the flowers you sent me
last Wednesday.
But since I am not alone
and words are here with me,
I wanted to let you know
that whenever you need love that flows freely
like the waterfalls in Castara,
in my heart is where you'll find it.

*Always♥*
*Prior, present and in our next chapter.*
.

**I couldn't let these words fall into the pit of my stomach.**
**I had to let you know that you remind me of the still fire of a sunset.**

Honey,
whatever may be tonight,
we cannot lock eyes.
That would be a beauteous disaster,
because darling,
we are playing in tender flames.
I cannot risk for my soul
to exit my body in a swift fashion
every time I re-discover your eyes.

You are walking temptation,
a drawing trouble,
*rock dipped in honey, dipped in gold, placed in fire.*
All the beautiful things that you are made of,
I would be forced to confess
them before your stare.
So to avoid the pressure
of desire asserting itself in this room,
can you please cease your mission
of seeking out my gaze?
Unless your intention
is for me to fall for you,
like irresponsible fruit
from a tree smothered in love.

If so,
*speak.*
All words and body language.
The space between us
filled with flora
and with fire.

But for my eyes to be lost in yours,
you would soon find out that
years ago,
you had me;
I am yours.
Like the feeling in your fingertips
as they graze the curves of my skin.
The fire in you.
I am yours.
Like your feelings
and the voice in your heart declaring a love,
although you are scared,
you still want more.
Like your *deepest, deepest* wish,
and your favorite song,
and that vision you had
night before last.
Like all those things,
baby,
I am yours.

The danger of your eyes in me
only means
that love is coming
to hold us up towards the sky,
like gold,
proudly and pleased
that we
have chosen to embrace
this wonderful emotion.

Darling,
gentle lover,
warm heart,
rock, roses, and rivers,
I am yours.

## There's perfect symmetry between my heart and that of a silver locket necklace...

In my eyes,
you're nothing short of an angel.
In the name of love,
can I see the beauty of your wings?
I say all of this as
I squint my eyes to look towards
the glorious light given off from
the circlet of your halo.

I have come here tonight
with enough emotion
to rebirth Big River.
There are few things
I cannot stay too long without:
the summer, words, and your warmth.
I love when you let the sun
sit on your shoulders,
while the day rests.
Paradise is
wherever you are.
(Look at what the sky has given me.)

I would be hiding the truth
if I say that
I am not moved to rejoice.
I'll sing for you;
some nights I'm musically inclined
and I can hear the harp playing.
Half spoken words
murmured under your breath.
We make beautiful music.

This room is a studio

**Isn't love delicious when its overwhelmingly familiar
and recognizable with your eyes closed?
Its like black tea with a spoon of brown sugar and a
hint of milk in the morning.
And nothing compares.**

I once heard someone say that
our shoulder blades
are simply our wings
that are brought to life once we become angels.
And lately I've been thinking
that I must be living in some sort of paradise
because when I look at you,
your wings,
they are out in their full glory.
(Your light,
it is gleaming beyond you
and I begin leaping in elation.)
I am so joyful that
I cannot conceal my smile.
I must be dreaming.

Did you know
that you are an angel?
Lover,
did you know
that you are a blessing?
Every time someone asks
where you're from you say,
"Brooklyn,"
quickly without even thinking,
but do you ever think to mention
Heaven as your hometown?

## Cornflower blue & fuchsia

Please,
watch the sunset with me tonight.
Not only to witness beauty,
but I want to tell you about love as it pertains to you,
while the evening sky conceals my eyes
that have borrowed from the river.

In comparison,
the beach is in love too;
a beaming, but calming love,
that frees the earth from its pain.
Have you ever seen
the way *ocean* clenches onto *sand,*
then releases,
only for a moment,
to run and tell the world
how mighty
the grit of the sand makes it feel?
Before the water has even professed love
onto the ears of every element,
it draws near to the sand once again,
for fear of forgetting what the heat of the sand feels like.
Do not take your eyes off the sand
as it forms up castles at the shore,
all to impress the sea.
With each wave,
the water gratefully accepts each one.
I watch them both talk in peace
after the high tide passes.

Love is beautiful.
And what is more beautiful than
the beach caught up in romance?
I've seen the waves blush,
turn away shyly,
but reach its hands out to cover the sand

in the gentlest embrace.
I've seen the sea somersault sensually in repetition
whenever the sand lays like gold under the sunlight.
Look at those granules of sun romancing the oceans,
displaying selflessness and loyalty,
by never leaving the arms of its lover.
After my observations,
I have concluded that this is the way to love.
Ask the people,
ask the beaches,
ask the mountains that rest confidently
under the skyline,
they will all tell you to
**love full or do not love at all.**

If I could not find another way to convey
the amount of love that exists in my heart for you,
in the many languages spoken amongst mankind,
I would invite you
to make the trip with me to Daytona,
so that if my words couldn't
balance on a scale alongside my emotions,
the visual would paint a scene
that would speak loudly enough for me;
boldly enough for me.

(You leave me speechless.)

You and I; like sand and ocean.
Born to love.
Let's build sandcastles in dedication
to the love we share
that will last beyond this life.

## I mean it

For when
the leaves have left the trees
and there are less things
existing in between my eyes
and the sight of you,
I will paint you a city
of your own liking.
All the things that excite you,
of everything that moves you,
of every light surrounding you.
I'll take a seat,
take my time,
prepare my paint and my humble canvas,
and paint for you
a city.

## You can place the flowers on the kitchen table and join me in the peace room

You must wonder why I stare at you so;
I am writing a poem.

Love is living in you darling.
It truly is.
Here we are,
finally living the lives we were destined to live.
Do you remember the very first years?
The beginning.
When we wished for a garden,
a beginner's planting ground,
but still a place to let our love blossom, nonetheless.
And the people,
the people surrounding us,
all in celebration of our love,
advised us to plant a tree that
yielded crisp, honey-golden apples,
that blushed red
and to wait patiently
for the shadow of autumn,
for them to show their faces.
And when the apples dangled
from the hands of the tree,
like gorgeous, jeweled chandelier earrings,
we were told to admire them;
to sit back in our courtyard
and enjoy one of the fruits
of our labor.
Love has a wonderful way of rewarding you
whenever you let it into your life to flourish fully.
Faith and fruition.

I am still in love with you.
The only thing that has changed
is the elapse of time.

My heart becomes oil
whenever you reach deep
down inside of your spirit and sing to me
a song orchestrated of cherry-red roses.
It is hard to believe that
you call those melodies mere speaking.
Your words:

- soft and smooth, like the brush over of *silkened* velvet.
- passionate and veiny, like the outer flesh of rosa gallica.

Sometimes I forget
what I had for dinner a few nights prior,
but there are some things that will
forever be etched into my memory,
like the countless evenings we spent on the beach
and whenever you came across seashells,
you would speak so much love into them.
And if I ever turned my back for a second
to wrap waves around my feet,
you would make music
of the conch shells,
and I would be called
right back to you.

Nothing has changed.
I'll never leave your side.
I love you like roses, I do.
If there is one thing
I know for sure,
it is that romance is red.
How dare they tie the hands of rage
to those of a loving hue like crimson.

For you,
I have denounced anger; sanguine is sensual.
For you,
to see red, is to see romance.

## Shadows of a dark red rose casted onto the living room wall

"What more could I ask for from love,
when everything I've ever wanted
is here with me,
nestled in my arms,
and I hope it never leaves me."
you say breathlessly,
in the midst of shoulder kisses,
as we lay like flowers
after a sensual dance.
The moon is spying on us,
so much so,
that it has begun to spill through the blinds.
I roll off of charcoal silk sheets to
make some tea,
that eases us more into the night.
Let us talk.

Did you know that this would be our destiny,
when we met that brisk, bone-rattling day
of my least favorite season,
when you were sipping coffee
as deep and as smooth as your skin
(espresso so deep and so smooth,
 that it credited your skin as its only muse of origin;
its main inspiration)
and I had only come to that café to
recite some poetry but I left with
a newfound knowledge of your name.
But tonight,
I'll call you honey,
or even sweetheart,
while you smile the same exact way
you did on the night that my eyes
were introduced to a walking blessing.

Yes you,
with the heart full of flowers.
Did you know that we would become
wide-eyed lovers,
begging the night to cover us in
love, love and more love?
Some days request 25 hours from me,
leaving me in a state of tire,
but as evening dominates the horizon
with a powerful drapery of indigo,
I make my way home,
two trains—
and a quick walk, four blocks west.
As I turn the key in the door,
I shed the remainder of the day
before I place my soles
onto familiar wooden floors.
You will be here soon
and I begin preparing for passion.

The screech of the kettle,
the creek of the house as it shifts
whenever the wind tickles its spine;
every sound fools my ears
into thinking it is the doorbell ringing.
I cannot wait to see you.
And I don't mean to be rude,
but hurry, please.
It has already been a day, my love
since I've witnessed the personification
of a reason to surrender to emotion.
But overall be safe in your journey.
And never mind the rain;
I know for sure the rivers of my heart
run more abundantly.

You ask me if I've been eating
ambrosia and fig again,
and I blush deep down in my bones.
This house speaks highly of you whenever you leave,
so I know that I am not the only one that misses you
when you are not here.

I have learned never to underestimate
the power of a forehead kiss.
You love on me until the rain outside
feels outshined and it halts at once.
It must be the free-flowing passion
relaxing in the arc of your eyes.
They call it emotion, don't they?
When you look at me that way,
those little sky fires up above draw closer to the moon.

## Lime, sour orange or grapefruit

When last have you eaten of love?
Not only the word, but the fruit.
The actual fruit
in its purest form.
Removed its skin
and eaten love's pulp.
Did you hold love like lemon
and squeeze it to make juice?
*I tell you,*
that's the best way to nourish your soul.

Did you pick it yourself?
Were you fulfilled?
When last have you
tasted fresh, ripe love
and ate until your heart was full?
Did you make a mess of your hands and face?
Although to you it didn't matter
if anyone seen love dripping from your fingers.
You didn't hide
because a fruit like love
cannot be concealed.
Love's rind is textured in melodrama.
Love would've yelled out from your closed palms
and stained lips for compassion.
We would have been called out to see you in love.

But were you nourished and content?
Or ever since,
were you left searching for more?
Has it been that long?

When you are good and ready,
the love is there.
And each fruit tastes different.
Each one fills you an entirely different way.
In due time,
you'll find a love you deserve.

(Love will find its way to you. Life is about three things:
love, lessons, and life work. All of these things are
promised. Love is selfless and kind to the heart. It is
effortless, but because it shouldn't be taken for granted,
it requires effort and work regardless. Love is for you.
Claim love as an energy source into your life. Through
love good things become great, and better becomes the
very best.)

## Bass

I need to slow down and listen to the music.
The lyrics still speak the truth.
The melody still explodes and
heads straight to my soul because
the music is GOOD.
It either makes me dance wildly
or feel deeply
until I'm fighting back tears
and chanting lyrics that
mirror the mood of my soul.

The music was:
- Falling for you.
  It was like the inevitable reoccurrence of the
  clouds being moved by the powerful entrance of
  summer, through the expression of tears,
  that falls down and becomes rainstorms from up
  above. And through this type of unconditional
  love, the Earth is fed, the plants are fed, and so
  are the waters and the people reliant on our
  beautiful planet.
- The way you spoke your entire heart through your
  stare before I was introduced to the passion living
  within you, through your kiss. Body language
  performed that sensually is a gift.
- The tranquility of summer nights. We would
  watch the sun as it ventured home for the night
  and the moon would take its place. We didn't have
  to say a word because the sounds of the night
  gave a speech fitting enough for the moment.

- How your touch warms my skin and I am left feeling like coconut oil carelessly left out on a countertop at room temperature. From sugar to caramel, that is the state of my heart whenever you whisper into my ear how deep your love for me runs. Each of your words feel just as pleasant on my skin as the summer does.
- How my mind will always be at peace where the sand and the waves become one body. I cannot explain it; I love the beach as much I do poetry.
- The first time we held hands.
  **Whenever we hold hands.**
- The sound of your laughter; the joy I'm met with when I see you smile.
- Whenever the hummingbirds chirp harmoniously after a morning cloudburst, as to announce the day is anew.
- How you walked right into my life like a living poem and pulled an infinite ribbon of words right out of my soul,
  over and over again; without explanation. You've inspired me to write again. If that isn't magic, I don't know what is.

**Be my muse...**
Lay one hand on my heavily edited manuscript on the minimalist, mahogany nightstand, as if it spoke the truth of a King and Queen reunited.
Lifetime after lifetime.
*And so does your other hand,*
*fall into routine,*
*and makes a familiar presence*
*at the dip of my spine.*

## Love has built a garden around us

Stay
with me;
with love tonight.
You don't have to
leave at the first call of
nightfall.
When midnight greets us with silence,
make a sound from the diaphragm
that resembles
"I love you"
and I'll turn an eventful evening
into a peaceful night.

I'll brew some tea
and we can sing your favorite love song
like we wrote the lyrics ourselves;
with feeling and with tears
welling in the corners
of our eyes.
Tonight we won't hide them.
This is mid-night emotion.
We can talk through our stares,
or if you prefer to speak,
do so from your heart.

I'll hush the tv,
put the fire on,
make sure you feel at home,
then write for you,
a poem,
and ask you to
close your eyes while I
recite to you
how kind your love has been to me.
(kind, patient, and selfless.)

And somehow our hands
will have found each other
and become intertwined like wild and carefree vine.
The night has a way of pushing you to seek
out your lover's touch.

**To have:**
Life in itself is love,
so if we do not **have** love,
then what do we **have**?
I am speaking beyond romance,
as in the type of love that
meshes with respect and peace.
Love for nature and humanity.
I must admit that I **have** lost count
of the amount of times that you **have**
stolen my heart.
I **have** looked for inspiration in many things
and you remain the most captivating.
Mentions of you in my poetry and
reflections of you in my paintings;
I **have** made you my muse.

**To hold:**
This year,
I have made resolutions
that I won't **hold** any grudges,
neither **hold** my tongue,
nor **hold** myself back with burden.
Maybe I am much more fearless than I used to be.
The clouds **hold** up the oceans above its atmosphere
and I believe that is an example of loyalty.
Please, **hold** me like I was your gold
or a dream you believe in.

Before you leave,
pause at the doorway and leave me with
a bit of romance,
as something to **hold** on to,
until you return.

Like wedding-like words,
to **have** and to **hold**,
above all,
it would be the hands of my lover
that I would choose
to be bonded to.

And there is love.
Not yours, not mine, but **ours.**
Every star in the navy sky above
smiles on us.
We don't have to let go.
Love loves us.

We don't have to say goodnight.
The night is for people like us
who love deeply
and leap trustingly;
who give their hearts fully.

I have flowers on the nightstand,
some words on my mind,
and patience in my heart.
I think tonight has been lent to us by magic.
I am here to listen.
Whatever you plan to say,
I will listen.

Tonight will be a good night,
just don't say goodnight.

## The little night words you utter

"Baby, don't turn off
the kitchen light just yet.
Leave tiny enough light
to capture the trace of a frame
that crosses me.
I'd like to see the evening art
that is draped over
your softened shoulder."

"Whether you sit in front of me,
or beside me,
just don't sit too far away.
It is past evening and
passion is persuasive.
Touch is tempting.
The night will marry us
when we sit in chamomile
and lavender like this;
using our midnight voices
and letting affection
make butter of us."

"Dim the light, dear—
but don't ever dim
your love.
I see so much in you.
If ever I look away for a second,
there is this fear buried inside of me
that I could possibly miss
a moment of what life is made for;
the things set for our eyes to see"

"Surprises after sunset
are something to
look forward to
because I've had a wonderful day,

but as the sunset thickens,
we still have love
to carry us through the night.
A river is a powerful
body of water in its own right,
but if it meets another river
of equal greatness and
joins hands in confluence,
then the beauty of their union
is also appreciated."

"There's no need to
strain your eyes
with the last promise of light
glinting from the window corner.
There's no need to
search for my face
in the heavy of the night.
Your fingers don't necessarily have to
dance across my face
to search for skin and teeth
to determine my mood.
Free your mind.
You won't ever have to
wonder if the dark skies chose to
conceal my expression tonight,
because as you may already know,
I have been trademarked with a smile
since the day I met you.
My eyes only see things in love now.
You wouldn't need the light
to prove how you
have bought along a wealth
of peace with you.
Thank you.

Everyone asks,
every place I go,
the reason why my soul is smiling,
and why I've brought all
of my dreams to the front of my eye,
and before I could move
my lips to speak,
they all answer in unison:
'LOVE'."

## Remedy

Honey and lime heals beyond the body.
"It's medicine" *they would say.*
Drink honey and lime to fix anything
and it will yield results.
So here I am,
wandering through the
narrow and crowded market aisles,
desperately in search of citrus fruit
and **honey,**
I am willing to give love a try,
if you are too.
Let's toast with an elixir
I know of,
that will wash down
the bitter taste of the past,
and that'll leave us speechless
all the way to the back of our throats.
I don't want to believe someone could hurt you.
How could they attempt to steal your good love
and leave without guilt stains on their fingerprints?
How could they flee a crime scene without
regret permanently sealing their lips?

Lime and honey.
Your love isn't theirs to keep,
it is retracted, recycled and reborn
to give to someone
of your choosing,
who loves you back
for the right reasons.

**Your happiness inspires Earth to continue in rotation.**
**(Go on and smile and inspire the flowers to bloom.)**

I could write about your smile all day.
When we are blessed with the gift of conversation
and I fall under the spell of your stare,
I see inspiration holding you dearly in its hands
and I begin writing an ode in my mind.

When you smile, it's genuine.
I have yet to know of something more precious.
Your smile makes me want to purchase
the finest cameras to photograph you
at your most joyful moments,
so you can see what it is I see.
So you can see what the world sees.

The very first time I seen you smile,
I searched and searched for the words
to describe what I had witnessed.
Something quite more spectacular than magic;
an expression of happiness written on your face
is just as special as the ocean.
And you never give a warning,
each time you use gestures
and body language to show me how
deep of a joy you are feeling.
I cannot count how many times
my heart has run off
and abandoned my chest,
in hopes that you
would catch it perfectly in your palm.
You touch souls when you
simply arch the corners
of your mouth upwards.

It is a simple action,
but little things like that
can change the world.
As you may already know,
I love roses,
fresh fruit
and beautiful words,
but I'm starting to believe
that there is nothing
more exquisite than your smile.

Please don't let anything
ever steal your smile.
Please don't let anything
ever steal that light you have living within you.

## Bouquet Ballad (I want love like...)

Rose.
Here are your petals.

(For the flower, life is never over.
When the pretty of the rose falls to the earth,
there is still life in the heart of the plant.
Rebirth and Regrowth.
O how you have returned once again to amaze mankind
and bring peace to this place!
We must rejoice for the roses.)

Everywhere you go,
you leave pieces of you.
Everywhere you go,
you bring along peace with you.
I must tell you,
every time you leave,
you are missed.
Wherever you have roamed to
and taken your love,
may you return to the heart that you call home.

(Rose stems and romance, and the patient wait for love.)

I cannot help but glance a wooden floor,
full of withered flowers and remember
the love that once lived here.
It makes no sense.
Pieces are missing.
Half of my heart from my chest.
Piece of my peace is gone.
*Dim daybreak*; the sun doesn't rise the same anymore.
*Muted midnight*; neither does the moon shine the same.
We are all in sorrow.
And all I can do is reminisce about flowers.
All I can dream of is running into your arms.

Whenever you come back home,
bring a garden with you.
I am longing for your presence.
Whenever you come back home,
bring the loyalty of the morning with you.

Like a faithful sunrise,
promise me
you'll be by my side
at the first kiss of light.

## Red rose & rhythm

So tonight,
I'll name the night after you.
Roses, cadmium red
and I wrote a song for you.
No words,
just tune,
just melody,
but it will say so much.
A song that will remain in our hearts forever.

And tell me,
do you feel the red roses
racing throughout this room
as we recite rhythm and romance?

All the love is for you.

## Great beyond words

There are plenty of skies
and many moons,
all painted in different moods,
but they do not
compare to you.
Even on the sweetest evening,
the sunset doesn't hold
a candle to you.
I've always been known to fall in love
with the resting sun
and still you shine brighter,
so how great does that make you?

## The dark

Like when current goes
and the lights are out,
all I do is sweat
and think of you.
(Without light, I can still see clearly that I need you
in my life)

After I lit the lanterns,
I drank some sorrel
to cool me down.
This heat
isn't the only thing
that has me heated.
My thoughts are on fire.
When you're looking to pass the time,
all you can do is sleep
and dream,
and when you open your eyes,
the lights will be back
like it never happened.

But still,
you aren't here with me.

(Dark nights on the hill when light has fled us.
Mason Hall, Tobago. Summer 2016)

## What is your medium? Forget it, I have figured you out.

You are an artist of the mind.

What do you do with a woman after you have dipped her
in sunrise?
When she has a pink heart, a blue mind, and a gold
soul.
When she is dripping bubble gum lilies and Georgia
blues,
and she's dancing on every cloud to her thoughts.
Do you love her deeply,
or let her go?

## Wasted Champagne

To say that I loved you
wouldn't have been enough.
*I love you* paints pictures of cliché love novels
with tear-stained pages,
flower petals sprinkled across silk sheets
and the hope for reciprocation.
And since what I felt for you ran deeper,
the definition of that feeling
is not yet in existence.
So much transpired over the years
and I became privy to
your lack of love for my spirit.
So it should come as no surprise
that I retired my love for you.

And the way I cared for you
may go down in history.
Believe me, I am scared to love that way again.
But I loved you,
loved you,
loved you,
even when the water came rolling in
and even in the dark without light to guide me.
I loved you like
mountainous rock holding up the sky
and never lowering their hands down for rest.
And I loved you like how flowers
hide their history in the dirt,
and that dirt,
how it clumps together and forms man,
in a second,
almost instantaneously,
it is gifted life and inhales passion into its lungs.
I loved you like that.
Until my soul would contract,
then release,

and lay weeping in my gut for the rest of the night.
Singers who serenade and move templates are poets,
and their words; poems.
Aren't they?
The timelessness of the lyrics flowing
from their mouths— like wine,
I know that they mean each word
that exits their vessel,
because they are crying a new emotion,
as they force their spirit to belt out the song.
That is love.
The kind that is placed inside of us before existence.
I loved you that way.
Remember,
I loved you like the night
and all of its sounds.
When the sky tears up and releases sexy lightening,
while it drops the linen overlay.
I would fall asleep counting the stars
imprinted in the sky
because the amount of lights
living above our horizon is infinite.
I would submit to slumber,
naming the many reasons
why I loved you
that excluded vanity,
and I would write essays in my memory
of all the reasons of what I believed
to be the purpose of your existence
until sleep caught a hold of me.
But you had secrecy tattooed onto your shoulder.
And you sought after my heart without good intentions.
Through every emotional dagger thrown my way,
I fooled myself into believing
they could possibly be growing pains.
The best advice I have to give is:
Never accept anything that isn't normal
or that is unhealthy.

It will dissolve your soul.
Acid is not kind to the blood.

I know now that you never loved me.
I was just a pawn in a *dangerous, dangerous* game.
I trusted you because
it was you that I laid beside
as night fell upon us,
and I felt safe enough to shut my eyes until morning,
and it was you that I poured the
contents of my heart out to,
without fear of you using your tongue
to form a repetition of words spoken
that were only meant for your ears.
With deceit as your talent,
I stumbled over the blanket of falsification,
that you lead me to believe was our protection
from the brutality of the world.
Fugitive of the heart!
Because you didn't love me,
everything I offered in love
became a sacrifice for your personal gain.

When you sit amongst strangers
and talk poorly of me,
do you begin to believe your own lies?
Does dishonesty take a seat
to the left of you
to witness your tales?

## Phlebotomy

I am the fool.
Sometimes I believe we have unfinished business
because every time I start over new—
here you are again,
draped over my shoulder,
stringing along my fingertips
and whispering your wishes into my ear.
What you want,
I cannot offer you.

I am building a new home.
Bare; I'm emptier than your tea cup
when you've consumed all of its content into your soul.
*I am but a healing woman,*
regaining my strength after my heart
was used as a red carpet to a soul ungrateful.
But just like the city blocks
surrounding the place where you lay your head at night,
*you know me.*
So it shouldn't come as news to you
that I am not leaping mindlessly,
*heart-first* into romance rushed,
that is:
undercooked and served hastily,
lacking depth,
without substance; nor a foundation to build upon.
Bland and seen as a pass time.
We would be like life-size,
paper-body cut outs,
that would serve as place holders
until our soul mates finally roll in.
And why,
should we waste precious time
instead of focusing on healing?

When you're lonely,
you reach for me,
like a hand extended out to you
when your inner body grazes the ground.

Go out into the world and taste life.
Listen to my words.
Become free and touch the far ends of our universe.
It lives and breathes, just as you do.
Romance isn't the only type of love wanted.
There's more.
Dear friend,
impatient lover,
there's more.

**So sad that it's the people who leave, but the house**
**that stays to feel the sorrow of it all.**
**If only I knew that the home feels it twice as bad,**
**I would've sent trinkets from all the places I've been**
**since to keep its mind at ease.**
**What about the pain that has leaked down into its**
**concrete foundation and is trapped there forever?**
**Images of us breaking are now encapsulated in its**
**bones and I'm sure there are no words for it,**
**just haunting flashes of memories.**
**"Two people who loved lived here" it will say.**
**"Two people who loved."**

Why did you leave the front door open
when you left late last night?
Weren't you afraid of frightening things
making their way into our home?
Or were the things we fear the most
already living amongst us?
Like shadows dug into the wall,
do we address them and
ask them why they have formed a wedge between us?
Or do we live comfortably with the fear of losing love?
*What does it mean to you?*
You are sleeping soundly in the guestroom
and I
spend the last sip of my nights
in the master bedroom,
watching the cars zip up and down the highway,
listening to them hiss all night.
I wonder what they're prattling about.
As the cars race past the window,
like bursts of light,
I become inspired as I think who should leave first;
*them or me.*
**Them or me.**

And I wait up until dawn arrives to close my eyes because I feel less alone.

I could only ever live in the city now.

## The regret letter

Extremely unfamiliar with knowing how to love,
for him—
it has become second nature;
almost innate,
to leech onto all good energy in his surroundings
and to any open opportunity available.
A vampire.
Remorseless and *evilous*.
Check his heart; it runs cold.
If he were an apple,
you could trace the dishonesty to his core,
and he would be made up of bitter flesh,
that is off-putting to most, if not all.
Disloyal.
If I had known,
I would've ran to a safer place.
Not to another's arms,
but to solitude.
*Wicked games* and
someone will be left to feel it.
Trickery ran like foam from his mouth,
and untidy in his work,
he left others to it
to clean his mess.
And he would sing this song
whenever he tried to lure good people in:

*"Everything and everyone is deceitful. Just full of deceit. Immersed and floating in it. Soaked in it and capable of combustion when the fire is right. So don't be taken aback if someone you trusted like the night with your life, cuts you like fresh loaf bread. Just like hot, fresh, baked loaf bread, that is hypnotizing in aroma, so you won't feel it while you are distracted by the taste of false love prancing on your taste buds. You'll notice the scars on your skin years later. They will take sandpaper to your heart and scratch it down, and leave it raw and open to vulnerability. And this is life, and like heartbreak and the last page of the final chapter, it is for certain. Don't dwell on it, but it will come like a rain misbehaving."*

I'm sure this pre-written passage
was placed in his mouth by something
of an eviler existence.
I'm sure those words might make you think
he seen the world for what it was
and he was offering up love tonight.
But he was only reading from his warning label.
A poison, a poison, a poison, a poison, a poison.
He was telling you who he was,
but if you fell into the trap,
and was hemmed up by the ankle by a vine of lies,
don't beat yourself up too much.
I don't think you'd be held accountable
for the venom he'll insert into your life,
because you don't notice it
until it begins to build up bulky layers of toxicity,
that you'd have to peak your head above
to see brighter days.

It's never too late to close a chapter.

*Leave.Retreat.Heal.*

## Aisle 3

Him.
The one that came before you,
would've told you,
that when I decided to leave
when I had ENOUGH,
that he, too
came running back to me; his secret sun,
and collapsed at my feet,
and murmured a breathy and pitiful "I am sorry",
but it had grown too late.

After I had moved on and healed partially,
he went on to ask when next we would meet
and told me that he was free all through my season.
In his mind,
we would be beneath the sun
and me, under his spell.
No. no,no,no.
I'd opened up my heart generously
only to be bitten by the spite of heartbreak.
He said he longed to see my face,
but if he ever seen a glimpse of me
it would only be in passing.
(O he was bitter; ask me again and again,
I'd still choose the aloe plant over him.)
I'll treat him like glass;
I'll stare right through him,
and apply
my oxblood lipstick in the reflection of his skin.

It was a Sunday afternoon,
on the corner of Church and Flatbush,
that I noticed his presence amongst the crowd.

Surprised to see me,
he left the vicinity that he occupied
to catch up to me
to say hi.
With my eyes hidden behind shades the color of asphalt,
and my heart guarded by wisdom well-earned,
I walked away to avoid the drama
he had dragging at the heels of his feet.
We were separated by cold, unappreciated pavement.
He must've called
my middle name a thousand times,
but I was heavily distracted by
the echo booming from his soul.
Empty. Just void.
He yelled out to me but I
didn't give him the words he wanted.
I spoke loudly from my diaphragm and said,
"Don't you see these flowers in my hand?
Do you think these are for superficiality;
to produce charm,
only to draw you close or
to make you yearn for my skin,
when your heart isn't that fond of me.
I figured you out.
You like your roses in the dark.
You call them *baby,*
but you don't make eyes with them
when the sun is shining.
Goodbye,
you are causing the flowers to wither.
Leave all petals right where they are.
I will make art with them.
Ungrateful!
You could never appreciate passion, nor the painting."

Take heed.
Like you,
he treated me like a love forgotten,
so I forgot that I ever loved him.

**I don't ever want to have another conversation
about one-sided love.**
It is like making black cake and using all the energy you
have in your body to create something wonderful, then
watching someone snatch it from the oven a minute
after completion, and gobble it down before it has a
chance to cool.
It's robbery of the heart.
Trust, memories, and hearts
fall to the ground in tales of selfish love,
and everything resembles dried rose petals
caressing the sweet concrete.

**Please don't take me for granted.**
For reference,
he thought I would wait around
another year to recreate a sequel to a tragic summer.
I walked away
and vowed to never bargain with my heart again.
You used to promise
you'd never become
someone I
would consider rescinding my trust to.
No one deserves to
sit in the presence of heartbreak twice.
Once I am gone,
I am gone for all of eternity.
I gave you chances like
the many stars that reside in the midnight blue.

You had me on a level of loyalty that couldn't be defined.
I was there for you.
Like a lover
and a best friend,
I was there for you.

I am serious.
I am leaving, for my health.
My mind is mine.
You have managed to capture some of
the tiniest, purest parts of me
and I have learned to live without them.
But gone are the days
that I cater my actions to please others.
I know that you sense the bold energy
surrounding me,
and you have come to despise this version of me,
that speaks my truth fearlessly.
I fell for your spiel and I found myself
living out the worst scenes of a horror movie.
You didn't believe I would leave,
because I faithfully carried you
and your suitcases of deceit
for the span of a decade.
But I am done.
This soft-spoken woman will walk.
Go ahead and ask the one who let my romance
run out onto an open floor,
only to return later to try and salvage
the syrup that had remained.

But we don't let spills
sit around for too long around here.
We assess the damage,
we clean up,
we heal,
and we never look back.

## You found your niche.
## They call you when they want to destroy art.

Look at your hands!
You are capable of pottery.
You almost had me,
but I was too hot for your fingers to hold.
Look at the motion of your fingers as you mold me.
Mold me. Mold me.
To make a good girl look bad; terrible
(you need an entire summer).

Tender things need holding.
Our hands always seem to lock together,
like magnet,
and people are beginning to notice.
Warm hands.
You have warms hands
and you place them on my emotional body,
causing me to dance.
I have seen your eyes look calmly.
I have seen your eyes stare in desire.
I have seen your eyes glare in lust.
I have seen your eyes take charge of the room,
but I've never seen your eyes tell the truth.
Are there any words renting a room in your heart?
Speak up and say something honest for once.
Don't let the lies speak for you all the time;
there's no reason to.
After all,
you refer to me as honey,
but you don't regard me as your lover.
You don't even know the rules to your own game.
*You're gonna lose your friend.*
Put your pride aside.
*You're gonna lose your friend.*
Even if we subtracted the heavy emotions,
you still could've saved a spoonful of respect for me.

But damn.
You've been holding back.
You must've been taking some art classes secretly.
An amateur, yes—
but you know a few things.
*My, aren't you quite the creative!*
You dealt with me like clay.
Calculated in your actions;
hands and mind working away
to create something most pleasing to you.
Unfold. Mold. Let the sculpture set in form.
And there was a point that
you were sure that you had me,
but I have been studying fine art for years
and I can read the message behind your creation.
I don't respect your intentions.
Come on,
even though the sun is vex
and is expressing itself angrily up above us
for the deceit committed,
don't let that distract you
from the fact that I would have **never**
risked your trust that way.
You made a mess and it has become *messing around.*

On August 27th,
the sky cried for us.
We had gone too long without a good rain.
The desert in your words
confirmed that it was all just fun for you.
When all the planets aligned,
so did thoughts of you.
In my mind.
You had me...

When loneliness haunts you this summer,
**don't call my phone**.
And when you are feeling creative,
I will not serve as your medium.
Please move on and make art without harm.

## Last time revisiting this feeling

This evening,
the memories are hovering over me
and won't ease up.
Maybe you are somewhere
switching the radio station as well,
before the songs that were once stitched into our love,
take us back to a place
we both forgot we had lived.

10 years prior.
Afternoons swallowed by fog;
it would rain
and rinse away the sunshine.
When our lips would become reacquainted repeatedly,
like each time was the first.
Absent were words,
as we had everything we wanted in our hands;
each other.
Back when we would cry
for things we never spoke about.
Your hands always seemed to find mine
and we stopped caring about
who witnessed our connection.
That is when we began living.
When summer knelt at our feet
and surrendered itself to us;
the warmth was ours then.
When I missed you all through autumn,
and by wintertime,
I decided I would never speak your name
from my mouth again.
Realize what you lost.

At some point,
we all learn that
whatever it is that the heart yearns for,
the mouth must profess,
before love gets up and leaves you.
Before you lose something
that was too good to you.

Pride ruins lives,
it ruins hearts.

I heard you were looking for my love,
when the flowers began blooming.
You remembered the way summer claimed us
and took us for the ride of our lives.
The shock of the thrill;
you wanted more of that feeling.
Maybe you wanted to sit under the sun with me,
until our skin became more heavenly,
and we would somehow continue
where we left off,
like I had not learned to live without you.
I don't think you know how perilous this game is.
Even to this day,
there's a particular song that
hasn't shook off the memories
of when my heart was yours.
Each time I get caught up in the music,
I must remind myself that my heart is no instrument.

The heat,
90 degrees
and my perm didn't stand a chance against love.
A lot of lessons learned.
*The **want** for things you don't understand...*
and my eyes only yearned for silhouettes of you.
Love is supposed to feel explosive,
but not like an addiction.

Couldn't get enough of your love, regardless.
**Magnet** *kinda* love.
Kissing 1,000 times,
within the span of 1,000 steps
towards your front door.
The way you effortlessly called me babe.
Summer 2009.

For old times' sake,
do you remember our summer,
and how I was red clay
within warmed, loving hands,
for you?
When it came to you, I was heated honey.
I was warmed-over sugar aging into caramel.
I was the pure silk of a midnight voice
whispering beautiful words to their sweetheart.
Like the flame building beneath a mild, whistling kettle.
Like the delicate fall of a petal from its floral body,
I was mid-poem
for you.
(I cannot believe I am finally writing this.)

I am back in my city
and I think I may stick around for a while,
so I'm sure someday I'll glance your face
in our small town; on a busy street.
I'll blend in with the music
and flow past you,
like I don't know the truth
behind the tenderness of your kiss,
or how you reveal your truest self
when you are most comfortable;
when no one else is around.
How you move like music,
when the sun descends.
Like I don't know of a few of the things that you love.
Like I never loved you.

## Take 1

You fear me now,
because I,
made myself into a wild and fearless woman,
when you thought I was washed down to nothingness.
I am not over.
This is my beginning.
Wait for it.

## Take 2

I can see in the mirror of your eyes
that you are aware of my rebirth,
and you never thought you'd see the day,
when I lose it completely
and begin doing things carelessly.
**A woman who learned to trust her garden
is one you should look out for.**
I have only shared with you ¼ of my mind
and you cannot handle it,
so you grab your belongings
and disappear into the night.
*As you should.*
You do not recognize me standing up straight
and staring you in the eye.
*How bold of me.*

## Take 3

Never run from the truth.
It will chase you down until you are breathless.

You think that I am smiling,
but I am sucking my teeth.
I am gathering all the right words under my tongue,
for when you,
and for when others
decide to try this *quiet-natured and delicate thing.*
I will have words
for anything that is working against me.

Label me a stubborn woman.
I dare you!
I wonder whether you've noticed,
or maybe you don't care
that I am tired and fed up.
You don't love me, *love.*
You've never loved me.

What you took from me,
is more than I had to give
and if you can live with that murky truth,
swimming in you and not see your wrongdoing,
then I must let this thing rest for good.
You know why I left.
But do you remember,
when I asked you in the summer
to help me cut the lawn,
because the flowers were buried
beneath the greenery
and I could no longer see their faces.
They needed to be saved,
but you shrugged me off
because to you,
I was no longer a concern of yours.

But when the snakes arrived in numbers,
you showed not one drop of emotion—
and then I realized
that the sharp, unruly grass
was something you grew straight from your soul.
It was your doing.
You brought your burdens here.
Your middle initial; does it also stand for serpent?

If you are going to speak ill of me,
you cannot do it here.
**Not in my home.**
Not where the flowers can hear you
lying through your pretty smile.
You have to leave,
by choice or by truth.

## The Dedication

I knew you were waiting for this.
You've always thrived off of attention.
THE DEDICATION.

If you peer past my skin,
beyond my blood,
and under layers of shattered heart (shaped like icicles),
an unpopular thought roams around
quietly and uninvited that:
what if I stayed with you throughout all of the chaos?
What if I gave you yet another chance,
for the hope that this time we would make it?
But I cut out the naivety,
and let out a laugh from the depth of my diaphragm.
You cannot out-love the wicked.
You cannot romance the cold-hearted.
What would I have been saving?
What would I have been fighting for?
There are no victories to claim when
you are out here fighting for a love solo.
You allowed me to feel alone
when you were somehow always there.
Even in your presence, you were never present.
*Your back turned to me,*
*like I was your opponent.*
I thought we were on the same team.
If only you fought for our love,
like the way you fought against my heart.

What a surprise that this tragedy didn't break me.
Each day I face the sun,
wishing for a day that would usher in
peace and renewal.
Never hopeless.

Love's last name is still written in cursive
on a little white label,
on the mailbox reserved for apartment 4B,
right outside of the corner apartment of my heart.
I will not let bitterness take over my spirit.
All of these stages were important lessons.


But I know that you break everything you touch.
If you had the world in the bowl of your hands,
you would upturn the globe,
break it up
and ignite its seven pieces for your own amusement,
then proceed to run for cover
to save only yourself.

To stay in torture,
would I even be here today?
Would I even really be here today?
Everything happens for a reason.
Those words are so true that they put fear in me.
If your heart wasn't a vessel for love to flow through,
exactly what emotion was pumping through you?
I thought that our union would've been
my first and last,
so I poured an abundance of love over you,
even when you donned a blizzard-cold shoulder.
I was so hopeful things would change.
Months before leaving,
I searched the entire house
for the love that I believed could've been misplaced.
But the love died like cheap, old bouquets.
The love died like the flowers in the backyard,
that you turned your back on.
Don't say I never tried to save our love
before it withered and become dust.
Aspirin saves clipped flowers in vases,
if only it did the same for tattered relationships.

Farewell.
To the parts of me you stole, keep them.
The memories, do away with them.
That woman you once knew, no longer exists.
She has since broken down
and rebuilt into something
you would fear:
a bold and lawless body of words.

## I despise horror movies after living in a terrifying reality of trying to love you

You would say that I
was not the finest petal encompassing the rose,
and that my petals were lackluster
and unimpressive to the eye.

I,
your last choice,
but your first conquest,
will soon overthrow your ruling,
because you fucked around and made an island of me.
The blueprint of pangea imprinted in my mind,
while I drift away from you in grief,
singing the anthem of an independent spirit riled up.

You held me beneath your midsection,
above the knee,
but far enough back
so I couldn't be seen.
And lastly,
you let your rage
put flames all through me,
to a point that
I have to wonder,
how am I still here?
How am I able to still survive,
thrive,
after all the deceitful digging up you did
to my roots and everything I planted?
You wicked son of a bitch.
You don't love flowers.
What you love is watching the honest bits of nature die.
But don't you rejoice just yet.
Even though you regard roses like weeds,
for which you have no need,
I am still here.

Look me in my eyes.
I am not a ghost plant.
I have not withered over and dried down.
I am not past tense.
I am here;
walking into my redemption.
This is my revival; I am claiming it.
And something is happening.
I feel a moment building in my spine.
Watch me make a performance
of grinded rose-meal and such.

*When a person sets out to destroy flowers,*
*to eliminate them from this earth,*
*when they result to ripping apart their essence*
*and studies them to recognize their flaws,*
*so that they can use their research*
*to knock them down to a level of superficial*
*submission,*
*asks them daily to be more like violets and*
*hydrangeas,*
*but not overly vibrant,*
*to confuse them a little further,*
*then lights a fire underneath their peace*
*so that they will live uneasily,*
*belittles them to nothingness,*
*and after the trauma,*
*watches them crumble and sift into powder,*
*then adds water,*
*and watches them through binoculars,*
*as they bubble and thicken in utter anguish,*
**is someone living without empathy**
**and a soul unfamiliar with love.**

So you want me gone?
I will not dissipate.
Every time you hold a bouquet in your arms,
you will flinch and begin to think of me,
and each flower resting within your fingers
will let loose a potion of everlasting memory
that will seep into you (skin deep),
and your spiritual mind
will have flashbacks of my displeased face,
and of me back-packing all the sacrifices I made,
that you comfortably ride upon;
like a carriage of gifts undeserved.
*Every time the velveteen dressing of a rose*
*tumbled to the gritty pitch,*
*you tuned in with deep interest*
*as my eyes flooded over in precipitation.*
Not another rainstorm from this body over you!

**Roses stolen —**
**regain their sugar rapidly,**
**and store their loving**
**in their stomachs away from greed,**
**so even if harsh, wintered people**
**cross boundaries and**
**approach their floral collectiveness rather closely,**
**their thorns will bite back.**
**And anything written for a rose**
**could never be erased,**
**even when evil wishes for the stunt**
**of its next bloom.**
**Your *wicked, wicked* ways**
**will never**
**have a chance to flourish here.**
**All your bad-wishing, baby**
***will never fall on me.***

**You know where we came from and all that we been through. Why would you...**

One step away from losing my shit and asking you to square up.

## For the record, I tried until it nearly killed me

It was over a long time ago.

I felt it in my soul.
It rested on my mind.
It wrestled with me in silence.
It kept me up some nights.
It worried me deeply.
It hid beneath our bed
and it emptied my pockets of hope.

## Lace

Seduction is not only for the body;
it was also created for the mind.
When I speak up for once
and you call me crazy,
but you know deep in your belly that I'm right.
Even at night,
as you rest in bed,
my voice lays down sensually on the chaise,
alongside the king-size bed
and replays like a love song that you cannot hush.
That too is seduction;
a voice telling the truth.

# **When exactly did you love me?**

I am still.
Each year I wash down into
a more diluted version of myself.
I mouth to you across the makeshift dining table,
*that I am half of myself,*
until my lips are sore.
I am fading,
and your lack of concern boggles me.
This life is repetition.
This pain is a cycle.
I think you might've built a house on top of me,
and I am tired because
the foundation is resting on my spine.
I am sorrowful because
I don't think that this home is meant for me.
My palms are caving;
threatening to slip and drop the mess you've made.
My wrists; trembling—
but I do not burst into a river
yet…

How many more years, dear?
How many more years do you think I have in me?
You shout *"nil!"*
as you leap from the *sueded* black futon,
and the remote skates into a corner.
The footballers shuffle across the screen
and you recline into the chair again with ease.
"1-nil"
you whisper,
as you look at me
with an emotion
that is intimidating to hate.

*Catenaccio, my darling. Catenaccio.*

## Sofa

Don't you ever break a body that is building.
I could tell that you've lost
respect for things under construction—
but never seek out my peace,
just to bring it to a place of unrest.

You have become too comfortable.

## There will soon be no one left to fight

Bone
bites back harder
than the bursting of a cold, jagged concrete.
Every time you speak
and
you are not in favor of,
vile condensation forms at the mouth.
You yell
and scream *red* until you have your way.

But these ways are gravel.
They are sharp and
have the ability to puncture through hearts.
Empty your pockets
and forget you ever had them.
Where we are heading,
we won't need them.
They will become a liability.

## Expiration Date

Go ahead.
Write how you really feel about me,
across my back,
as I turn to leave.
This body is leaving.
If I want to live,
I have to.

Do you even see me anymore?
Or in your eyes,
has my body
just become a shell;
a statue that you have placed beside the furniture.
You don't even look at me anymore.
You don't even bite your tongue
as you overindulge in wicked words against my being.
Haven't I done enough?
I have absorbed so much poison over the years,
because it was tasteless
and I couldn't detect its damage,
until it hit my bones.
Look at me as I fold over,
like old, hoarded papers,
like a photograph smoldering
from the corner up.
The flames beat up against
its body and rename it as ash.
Well,
I am breaking now
(to dust)
and I cannot stand up any longer
if I stay with you.

My dear,
I am hurting,
and it is selfish baby,
to not love me,
but still want me around.
I watch you sometimes,
*comfortably serenading other flora in front of my eyes.*
The respect is gone,
and I do not wish the sight
of one witnessing their lover
picking wildflowers over faithful roses,
on anyone.
It burns the throat, like whiskey.
Like a solo game of handball,
before dusk,
in the neighborhood park—
that big, bad ball of hurt and betrayal
will jump out in front of your face,
while you continue to keep dodging it,
until the day you wake up and realize
you've spent almost all of your love currency
on the wrong lover.
It'll keep you up at night,
and it replays in the mind,
like bad decisions
and a list of regrets.

You are so confident that I'll never leave,
but one day,
all of your love crimes
would eventually form a book
and place itself before me.
One day my eyes would read the pages
and realize this isn't good for my blood,
and I would have to escape.
When I think about our beginning,
and how much I stomached
because I loved you,

I could only describe this whole thing as a tragedy.
I feel sorry for my body—
to watch it forward through the years,
all through my memory,
left alone to battle agony.
Each scene stings my flesh,
like it intends to punish me
for ever loving you.

Just tell me tonight,
(before I lay my head down for well-deserved rest)
that you never loved me.

I'll sleep better.

Please.
Don't watch me while I dream,
because it wasn't easy to find slumber.
I breathe the deepest sigh at the slightest peek of dawn,
and then collapse into dreams that exist
as anything but sweet.

I didn't know you were fond of
drying out flowers,
instead of loving them while they were alive;
while the love is still beating in them.
Close the room door, please.
Whisper before you turn your back,
while you pull the gold door knob aggressively,
that you don't love me—
Not anymore.
Never before.

## Golden ticket

Why didn't you leave me to the wolves?
*Tell me a lie.*
Make sure to whisper it into my ear,
like a sweet secret,
so it would be certain that
I would follow you to the end of earth.
My body might as well be wooden décor.
I take a back seat to everything else...
Every other being similar to me,
lights your *candled* eyes.
Every other being like myself,
except for me.
But I have learned to eat my tongue
because you deny it.
You deny it,
like it is eating you from the core.

Learning to live with the fact
that they never loved you,
although you loved them like
fruit loves the ground **(destined and always returning),**
is not something to live with at all.
Leave it and flee,
before the poison kills off your love.

Why didn't you
leave me to the wolves,
or to a beast who would've clenched its teeth,
before telling me
who they really were before war.
But you preferred to lie so delicately,
that my heart sapped it up like a kitchen spill.
Pomegranate woman.

You've been sharpening your tongue again,
and
*oh* do your words cut;
*they cut me so.*
Agony is eating away at me,
and for the life of me,
I cannot comprehend why
the *life of me*
is tumbling to the floor.
Contents and dignity,
while you invent a new way to dig into me.
Anyone could see that
you are beyond innovative,
as you pull apart my romance
and turn it into spiritual revenue.

**You should have left me to the wolves.**

## The river is not in my eyes tonight

♪*La-lala-la-la-lala-la,*
the ever-observant moon,
*la lune,*
is listening.
It is not me—
who is crying tonight.

The stars are watching us like eagles tonight.
So focused,
like they have made risky bets on our behalf.
It is not me—
who is breaking this silent evening.

Tonight, I will celebrate my strength.
Crying over you only exists in faded memories.
I have washed my hands seven times clean of you.
**I am done.**

## Discard the poison,
## but sometimes the wound still hurts.

Once in a red moon,
I become too scared to look in the mirror.
A pair of worrisome pupils
takes me back to this one instance,
when someone tried
to hide their own fear in me
and I fell for it.

Have you ever tried removing poison from your flesh?
It self-identifies as a parasite.
The healing won't be pretty,
but I'll fight through it.
I dread the nights when the mirrors in the house
pierce past my skin,
and I am forced to keep my eyes thrown over my
shoulder.

## Roses that grow beside the waterfall

Soon,
when the rain falls,
I hope that it falls heavy.
My hair will give into the elements.
Rosewater will run from my skin,
like watered-down paint on a canvas.
Every fruit from my mind, will turn to wine.
My clothes will become drenched and trace my body.
All of my dreams will mold themselves
into the statuettes of my new reality personified,
and I won't want for much more.
The best part is that no one will notice my tears,
as they would think
they are sweet raindrops.

Let me share with you the type of rain
that I've been praying for.

## The same

And I don't want to hear that you
believe in
roses, green roots cultivated in fertile soil, and romance,
now that rosewater has found its way to your skin,
and you now walk a road of velvet petals, *rouged* red.
To see it as it is,
from the beginning,
is the actual magic.

Everything you love now, has been.

## Let the petals blow in the wind

There are certain things I cannot forgive.
If you have ever stood in the way
of my progress,
my growth,
teared me down to weightless petals
and watched me fall like saddened rain,
*then you do not love me like you say you do.*
There's something you need from me,
so you keep me around for eternity.

I need to know:
Don't you want me to be beautiful?
Don't you want my flowers to bloom?

**The many ways I broke, but I am mended.**
**I am somewhat better now**.

It did.
It crushed me.
Stone, candy, and ice.
But I am water.
I'm water now.
You cannot contain me.

## Yes, the R train goes into Queens.

Did you choose her?
The silent and wild-looking one,
sewing words into her palms.
She has crossed too many rivers;
too many fires to get here.
She will not ruin herself for the likes of you.
Besides,
you do not want to dip sunflowers in honey.
You will not be able to contain it.
It may be too much,
**too much,**
for you to handle,
since its evident that
your intent is superficial.

Leave that woman alone.
She is healing.

Empty lust and gluttony walk hand in hand.
They are inseparable and
they both possess egos that are revolting.
You have no interest in her mind,
so why is it that you want her?
You do not know.
In one glance,
she can already detect
that you are unready.

Leave that woman alone.
She is healing.

## The Remedy

Rest when you have cried once with tears and twice
without.
Rest when you feel like the entire room.
Rest again when your load becomes too much to bear.
Rest when you have healed entirely.
Rest when you find peace.

# December

**I must be a flower.**
Deep into my dreams,
someone whispered in my ear,
that each time a flower is picked in the name of beauty,
we rest it before our eyes
to bring ease to our senses.
But as the flowers approach their *closing curtain,*
how do we make sense of plants
that are losing their summer?
We take the very best parts of them
and plant them again and again
in good soil.

The dream collapsed,
and left me with a continuity
of silence and contemplation,
and I knew then
that I was a flower.

The heat.
The heaviness of the heat came in
and became a thief of my energy,
but I've learned how to deal with it.
Even when my spirit
fights to not fold under
the blazing sun,
like galvanize,
I still remain focused that my season
is soon approaching.

The rain.
The rain washed upon the silky dust
and birthed mud,
for the people to trek through in my village.
It keeps us all grounded.

I've learned that we must make sacrifices for the rain
because it brings about so many blessings.

*(How to bring a rose back to life: replant. add love.*
*add water. some of that sun. more and more love.*
*the quiet, positivity, optimism, and unshakable*
*faith, all while I relearn the importance of a mouth*
*full of prayer and its impact on a soul tumbling*
*through life's lessons. I am a flower in search of my*
*roots, but I rejoice even in the closest things that*
*feel like home)*

I've taken two glances in the mirror
and I've confirmed that I am a flower.
I know what two years living in the ground feels like,
with crushed soil itching up against my skin,
like a barricade of sea-kissed sand,
clumped and formed,
like muscle
around me from the root up.
**(from the root up)**
Many of those days I couldn't move.
Stuck I was,
desperately looking for any beauty
remaining in my situation.

A home; a sanctuary—
is not a sanctuary at all
if there is no peace there.
A garden isn't a garden,
if we allow it to serve as a battlefield.
It will only be remembered as a scene of ruins
if we let misery move in.

And then there's chaos.
Precipitation from sunrise to sunset,
that settles in the belly of the gully,
and all of the crops rinse away as the earth floods.

Scornful droughts that make the days appear longer
and make us question our willpower to exist.
In both scenarios there is loss.
Plenty of loss.
But what about the aftermath?
I declare by this time next year,
I will be content.
The pain I endured
in the previous years,
will soon be outnumbered by happiness.
I am sure of that.
Anything in existence
that thought it had me defeated,
*never really had me,*
and will soon display regret
for ever trying to erase my story.

All flowers I have seen with my own two eyes,
that have bent their heads in a moment of defeat,
will eventually raise their heads,
way above the clouds,
with an infinity of pride.

## Robyn, be gentler with yourself

What a shame!
I almost forgot that I
had bones and that they,
along with a slew of other things
can break and shatter,
and that is when I'll miss them the most,
when they are considered gravel to sift through.
I cannot say that I speak kindly to my core.
I cannot say that I treat my skin gently.
I cannot say that I forgive myself often.
If I continue this way,
I will burst.

## Serenity

One of the reasons I cut my hair
was so I could easily rinse my mind
of every tragedy,
one by one.
Pain does not dissolve all at once.
Whenever it would resurface,
I quickly rinsed it all away by hand
and allowed my scalp to heal from the torture.
I would watch
all of my expelled mind
wash down the drain,
funnel-like,
never to make eyes with any of those
bad memories again.

Peace is a mindset.
I need it.
It is the only thing that I
would open my mouth and beg for,
because you can have everything
possible in the material form,
but if you don't have peace,
it all means nothing.
And I am not speaking for us all,
I'm talking from experience.
That is the story I've been trying to tell.
I am on my knees,
praying for the peace I deserve.

## *Mshairi*

Midnight hour.
Words and thoughts run through me
like cool whispers.
I repeat them. I write them. I release them.
And they don't stop.
They flow out of my mind like a high tide;
ride alongside me like harsh waves.
They burst through my mental dams,
like revengeful flood waters.
I do not silence it.
I somewhat embrace it.
Some of it as soft as feathers.
Some passionate as forehead kisses.
And some of it as painful as the prick from a needle;
tolerable but still felt.
They keep me awake.
They gracefully skip through my imagination.
They come to life before me
and prance at the tip of my tongue.
They escape the purse of my lips.
Those stubborn words.
And if I don't make note of them,
they flee like I've done something to chase them off.
(sometimes never to return)

I don't know what it is.
Those words,
are my words.
Those thoughts,
are my thoughts.
Are they meaningless,
or are they the answers to the questions I dare not ask?
What does it mean if words do not let you sleep?
What does it mean if you are a prisoner of prose?
Am I a writer, or a senseless over thinker?
A careless daydreamer?

I prayed that if writing was the solution to every problem that I have,
I would live my life through my words, my pen, and my voice.

## Survival

The way it has been for me,
internally,
*I feel like all of my bridges will fall,*
*all of my dams will flood over,*
*and each of my skies will storm.*

But I need all of my mind to be fully at peace.
I need all of my heart to succeed.
I need all of my soul,
so that I can walk freely into my destiny.

## Don't let it fade away

Why are the loveliest things
always the first to go?
Before we even have a chance
to say goodbye,
we are forced to watch them
leak and froth over.

Why do we have to lose,
just to lose again?

## More poetry

In this life,
if I only existed in the form of rhythm and voice,
I'd still write.
I'd write and write.
Even if I were without,
I wouldn't change.
I would let my tongue become a tired muscle.
If there ever came a time
that I
couldn't get my hands on paper and pen,
I'm not afraid because
the last breath of me
has been reserved for poetry.

## I wish peace for every poet

I am not talking to myself,
I am displaying poetry.
I am revising the best fruits I have to offer.
Most of them,
like keepsakes,
have lived in me for years
and I am now reciting them.


(All the things you've wanted to say over the years,
write them down; sans structure.
Grab a notebook and make record of it, and see the
immenseness that can arise out of your deepest
emotions constructing their own city on the page.
This can be an effective form of healing.
No fear; leave it all on the page...)

## To praise or to put aside

Have you ever cut open a guava
and seen it taken over in worms?
Tell me why
have they left the ground
and invaded that body of fruit?
What will become of the plant's mind?
Is it peaceful,
or is it an encircle of noise?
And most importantly,
is it worthy?
Yes.

It is still sweet and able to make juice.
It never fell from the tree
and it upheld its grace throughout.
So maybe all is well.
My aunt's neighbor would rip open guava
from her tree
and dispel the worms,
like bad thoughts,
one by one.
They didn't seem to bother her any.
Some might say the guava
was half-bad and to do away with it,
while she believes the worms sought out
the guava because it was so mighty,
that it would be an honor to be in its presence.

## **Pure**

Take my hand.
We are all we got.
There's time for the world to repair where it's hurt you,
I promise.
I know a place where cold hearts regain warmth and are
washed clean again.

(And I hope you choose happiness. That is the path that
I am heading towards. *I know, I know* the pain you were
forced to carry. I hope that you find healing and I hope
that love finds you real soon.)

## Alaska

I can see the ink spills
of where some have failed to love you.

It's been written.

But it is never over, until it is over.
Pass me a pen.
I wish to write you a poem of peace.
I would love to see you living
with a little more roses surrounding you.

## When the world seems heavier, just know that I got you

Calm
and cover in mauve and midnight.
*Tonight is your own.*
*Tonight is your own.*
*Tonight is your own.*
Spend the evening how you may,
and anything left over,
all the moments succeeding the sunset,
allow me
to continue on in the art of renewal and love.
I will tend to tomorrow,
you focus on the feeling,
and I promise to prepare what is needed for healing.

Here's your tea and lavender oil.
If peace is with you,
your patience will never leave you.
And we have all been to a place like this
and overcame.
If you have ever felt **it** in full,
then you know.
If it is uncertainty you are feeling,
you can speak to me about it,
because you are never alone.
But baby,
we are chasing the sun.
What is for today,
will be.
Even if it resembles pain,
don't stare at it too long.
Put it to rest.
When you wake,
we can fix whatever is causing you to lose sleep.

## Prototype Un

He plays the guitar
as he asks her "What is your life work?"
She smiles as she shuffles past him.
*Magenta ribbons crossed over her ankles so elegantly.*
The way she walks is a gift of grace.
To deny her flair,
would be a disservice to the truth.

Today is a dedication to her.
*When last has there been a song for her?*
**And the guitar plays louder.**
The musician begins to sing,
and she is empowered by
the wedding of lyrics and tempo.
*To her there is nothing better than lyrics and tempo.*
There is a floor cushion positioned
in the middle of the room
surrounded by a rain of rose petals.
This space is hers.
That woman.
Never underestimate her.
She is dainty and delicate, yes.
But her mind is as powerful as the oceans;
her mind is as open and vast as the skies
that are decorated in clouds.
Her heart is molded from the finest love.
Leave your judgement at home.
She is the only one who defines herself.
A woman of many dimensions and layers;
*each one will take your breath away...*
The strums of the guitar brings her to tears now.
She is emotion.
She is the most creative and artistic being
walking this earth.
This is indisputable.

Her tears are beginning to flow and
she releases strain from her shoulders.
She throws her head back and releases a sharp cry
that attacks the voice of the guitar.
Guitar and woman form an alliance and she begins
to sing now.
Those tears leak down to the roses.
They begin to soften and bleed now.
And here we have it,
this blessed woman is making rosewater.
She is pleased to see that her tears
have not gone to waste.
She quickly grabs a basin to collect her creation.
She kneels over the bowl to wash her face
in the sea of flowers.
She murmurs, "What is the truth?"

*Man playing guitar* is hypnotized by her mystery
and poise,
so he begins to play the guitar fervently.
The acoustic sounds like the perfect electric guitar,
and he begins to chant in between the notes.

Night is falling on the duo;
their eyes covered by the hands of evening.
She searches for the musician by the sound
of the guitar—
and he follows the scent of the rosewater.
Neither one of them reach for the light switch.
Look at the curiosity of the sky,
as it tumbles in nosily
through the windows
embedded in the brick walls.
Tender, quiet sky,
settling like a flat soft drink before our eyes,
laying down for the night,
wearing moody blue and blushing pink.
Her light is reminiscent of the sunset too.

Also calm,
also captivating.
The musician thinks there is no difference
between the two.
She is of nature.
She is not yours to create.
She is not for your entertainment.
Take your hate and place it elsewhere.
She was made for this world,
but not intended to carry its pain.

The guitarist raises up from his seat
and bends his back,
as his sings about how free the spirit of this woman is.
He breaks out in a speech of how we must respect her
and never deny her importance.
His voice is drowning out the instrument.

The room can no longer contain her
and she bursts out of the front door,
running into the street dancing and singing,
waking up her whole city.
The ribbons that once adorned her feet,
fall onto the sidewalk,
and passerby begin to collect the fuchsia, curly fabric
as a souvenir.
A legend has been here.
Here comes the man with the guitar,
singing soft *la la las* to compliment her live art.
The bowl of rosewater;
she sways it from hand to hand,
as she moves her feet in a soulful two step.
All of the eyes out tonight are on her.
She begins to pour wet roses over her crown
and proceeds to walk down the main road.

She is singing the words:
"First land, tell me more of your truth,"
and the sky starts shedding tears and releasing
lightning in handfuls.
Stars begin to dash from side to side above the woman,
and the man behind the guitar
follows her down the road,
as he covers her in uplifting words.
I wish that you can see her in all of her glory.
If you see this woman,
call out to her.
Let her know that her light cannot be erased.
Let her know that all of the sounds of earth
have been inspired by her.
Give her a reason to smile,
she enjoys laughter.
A belly full of humor will hold her over
whenever the pain of the world
becomes too heavy for her arms.
In that moment, hug her.
When you see this woman,
smile in her direction.
Tell her she deserves love
that matches the many centuries
she has witnessed through her eyes.
With eyes so brown and alive,
she can see all of your intentions before you've arrived,
so don't lie to her.
The fibs hurt past the bone,
so please,
just come in truth.

In case you have missed the sight of her,
she has danced across the entire city tonight,
bending her body over like bamboo,
hitting each move like she was a camera's muse,
dashing roses with water all across the town,
leaving the people wide-eyed and in awe.

She has come alive tonight,
with the help of the guitar.
As the hours fly by,
she does not cease.
She will continue this way into the day.
This is the way healing is performed.
She is a dancing woman.
A damn good dancer.
Carefree and untamable.
Some will say that
she's just making noise,
because they are incapable
of standing in silence
to listen to what she has to say.
But let them talk.
**You must project your voice above the static**
**if you have a message to share.**
What she has to say is so important.
Listen, please just listen.

You cannot restrain an element.
Her energy will not allow restrictions,
so please,
let her roam free.
Let her dance across this world as she finds her way.
Let her leap, skip, sprint, fly, saunter, fall.
It's okay if she falls.
But most of all,
let her dance.
This is important too.
Let her let loose.
Let her dance because she loves to groove.
Let the sax and trumpet set her in a trance.
Let the drums awaken her purpose.
Let the beat and the rhyme move her beyond her body.
And lastly let the sweet, sultry calypso soothe her.
Let her sweat.
Allow her to feel.

Let her be bad.
Let her be good.
Let her be free.
Let her be.
**This is of most importance.**

## Mirror

I am a lover.
I am a writer.
I am a writer.
I am a writer.
I am a poet.

Nothing can take that from me.
Nothing.
I am unsure of what life has in store for me,
but no matter what may come,
I am writer.
Nothing can rob me of my destiny.

Words.
They are beyond beautiful, aren't they?
Like heart, like stomach, and like lungs,
they are a part of me.
They give me courage to walk,
when I know that I am too weary to take another step.

Even if I lacked the physical tools
to record the art existing within me,
and I found myself in yet another bout of solitude,
I would speak my emotions aloud
and recite it back to myself,
in a simple *call and response* fashion,
because poetry begins, ends and reincarnates
in the mind.

## The sun will shine for you soon

Tender soul,
don't give up
because it's not done.
There's so much more.
There's so, so, so much more in store for you.

## Emotional

You are this way
when everything vibrates through you.
I can feel it ten times as deep.
So deep,
that I've become a feeling.

(My heart is *reddened* from rose petals.
I am overcome with the love I was put here to feel)

## Rise or fall

If I were to cave,
the time would be now.
It's been nearly a year.
Most of the memories have slipped away;
not by choice, but by survival.
Do you understand what I mean when I say:
"I do not recognize myself like this."
I am an image of a woman
that I glimpse on the other side of the street,
lost in time and stuck in fantasy.
*I do not know this me.*

If I were to make it,
the time would be now.
I'm ready.
I've been pushed past my limits.
I'm at my strongest.
I hear and see everything,
so I'm ready for whatever may come.

## Tender heart, strong spirit

What?
Were you asking if I was the rock or the rose?
Both.
And why?
Nature and circumstances.
Nature and circumstances.

## Hold my hand

Never to stray too far
from the things that we have come to love.
Poetry.
Like the moonlight to sleepless souls,
I need you.
I need you desperately.

Poetry.
Lyric. Lines. Loyalty. Love. Life work.

Never leave me.

Together we make magic.
Together we make music.

If there is no poetry, there is no peace.

## Peace and red roses (We will grow stronger)

You are not broken.
Come.
Build again.
I am with you.
We will never lose.
Experience is a gift.
I promise you,
in this life,
we will never lose.

## Bring the roses home

To anyone who has asked
where I've been
these past few years,
I have moved.
To a few cities. (None of them felt quite like home.)
What exactly is the definition of distance
to a woman on a journey?
I have begun using the word "far" way less
since realizing that each place
is never really far from anything,
because you can build a life wherever you choose.

Have the years been kind to you?
I hope your life work finds you
and that you discover the answers
to all the questions you seek in life.
How have I been?
I've been well. (I hope you are well too)
I will not let negativity narrate my story,
especially since things have been looking up.
Lately I've been spending full days in my garden,
planting flowers and such.
I bought some land
on the island my family hails from,
along the coast of the beach,
and I haven't felt such peace as I do now
living beside the bay.

I hope that life has been
a warmhearted confidant to you,
and that you get to witness all of the emotions
that the sky has to offer us:
- the energetic cornflower blue that we wake up to,
- the ever-reflecting indigo of the evening that
  questions this life,

- and the mystic violet that crawls in before we close our eyes.

It has been days,
months,
years,
and I do not know if I am a poet or a gardener.
A lady of flora or a writer.
Growing flowers in the ground,
or in your mind,
takes a lot of work.
Many times I have thought about
leaving this life alone,
but it would bring tears to my eyes
and rip away at my heart,
to see words and roses daily,
knowing that I gave up on my dreams.
**Never give up on your dreams.**
If you believe in something,
that is all you need.
Believe in your dreams,
and have faith that they will lay back trustingly
in the hands of perseverance,
and you will surely obtain everything
that is meant for you.

Life has a way of shaking up the reality
that we might've grown accustomed to,
and when change runs in,
we are set on a new path to begin again.
I know,
I've lived through it twice.
And if ever
change has cleverly spun you like a top,
just know that you are never lost,
you are actually finding your truth.

I hope that each time you have rebuilt
and reinvented yourself,
that it was as easy as placing your hands
in ocean waves.

Everywhere I go,
I will tell people,
I am from a city that exists as a village,
full of talented beings,
who use their gifts to uplift and to tell their stories,
and the way they talk is poetry,
where they live—
is an oil painting in a fine art gallery.
I am thankful for my city,
for teaching me
how to live with love,
wherever I go.
Beautiful, beautiful Brooklyn.
East Flatbush *everlasting*,
thank you for your gifts.

## Faith

I spent way too much time planting the seeds,
that I wasn't sure if I even believed
I would see flowers appear,
but it was the dream that sustained me.
I am amazed that roses have shown their faces.
There's a blessing hovering over me.
There is fruition after falling.
There is a love novel after 7 bad horror stories.
It gets better.

This field looks 75 percent full,
but I am still pleased.
It is the growth that I am proud of
and I don't need validation for that.
Some mornings
I can't believe that
a humble rose woman like I,
ventures out into the world
to buy soil and to fetch water.
I won't lie,
some days I want to be alone,
but there are things I must do.
But all of this labor that I have done thus far,
all of the earth that I have turned up
in search of the truth,
was not done in vain.
Please,
let this woman
enjoy her rose garden.

I want to enjoy my garden.

## Rosewater Prelude

What do my neighbors think of me?
Every morning,
I set a jar on the windowsill
and wait for it to fill up.
There's something trickling down
the exterior walls of my residence.
It is not rain.
There is a rose vine that is written
in cursive above my apartment.
If you came to visit,
you would see mason jars placed off in a corner,
filled with fluid the color of cherry blossoms.
Every time the light shines into my living room,
each container glistens.
I do not understand
what exactly I have in my presence.
It ripples like an ocean
inside of its transparent encasing,
just by the slightest sense of movement.
Even with being encased inside of glass,
*this magenta show*
is causing my house to smell heavenly.
There is a hypnotizing fragrance escaping through
every crevice of this home.

Last week,
someone I once loved
showed up at my doorstep,
with faux flowers in their hands
and a mouth salivating with fibs.
While they babbled,
I didn't attempt to chip in.
I looked beyond their shoulders; into the valley.
Due to my silence,
he put pressure on his oxford shoes
and turned away to skip down

the concrete flight of stairs,
lined with flowerpots.
The thought came to me
to wash down my doorstep
with the water that favored guava flesh,
that I've been harvesting.
With one dash of a bucket,
a blush waterfall covered the ground before me
and I haven't seen the feet of my former lover
on my porch since.
So this thing—
given to me;
a byproduct of scarlet red roses,
propped above my window,
is a remedy for peace?
You mean to tell me,
it is a symbol of change?
I don't know what to call it.
I call out to each of the ten roses that live above me
for the meaning of this gift.
Nine of them turned their heads and faced heaven,
but the one closest to my ears whispered:
"Eau de rose."
Eau de rose?
"Oui."

-

## Remnants of Rosewater

Everything came all at once,
like an abundance of rose petals,
but not as romantic,
and certainly not as pure.
Not a touch of softness to set glow to my skin.
The rain came too.
You should've seen it.
Both were heavy.
Both had the ability to wash away my entire being.
I have seen men swing their cutlasses
at sun-dried coconuts,
for the purpose of nourishment;
a determination to remove its shell
and release vulnerability.
It was this way that the storm hunted me.
**Like food**.

I'd given up,
I'd given in,
and I'd laid down
and let tragic rain and tormented roses wash over me,
like it was trying to take me as a casualty.
I left my home, my body, to witness my rebirth.
Never have I seen such a beautiful pain.
Somehow, I couldn't escape my garden.
There were rose petals swelling in me like rice,
dancing in my lungs like air,
nestled in my stomach like food,
and filling my hips like a soca rhythm.
They were entangled in my hair like clips.
I bawled out,
and only roses left my lips.
Pink. Orange. Red. White.
Fragrant and sweet, but of misery and of heartache.
So colorful, yes.
And they cut so deep.

There was pain,
but I knew that nature had its work to do,
as so did I.
The mystery of what was taking place,
inside of me,
spiritually,
could only be seen internally.
Not with eyes, but with the heart.
A sugared, sweetened rain that refused to cease.

The only version of myself that I am familiar with,
is that of an innately hyper-creative soul,
that has always been resourceful
with the tools that I'm left with.
The aftermath of it all was the decision to make
Rosewater!
*Something promising after the countless storms.*
Soak the roses.
Infuse the water.
Things take time.
This is a healing process.

I shall make rosewater for my sisters.
I shall make rosewater for every woman
who has come a long way,
whether physically on foot, or emotionally.
For the women on a journey,
I celebrate you.

I will make rosewater for my grandmother,
to heal her heart.
She doesn't cry,
but sadder emotions also visit her,
just the same at times,
as they do us all;
her children.
She was born a businesswoman,
so I know she will also use it for profit.

She will double it,
and distribute it amongst our relatives.
She will send it to our birthplace.
Her children, grandchildren, and great-grand,
will make do with it,
and it will be something to bring us all closer.

Rosewater for my mother.
She will use it as a toner to care for her skin;
a new addition to her routine.
Mom, above everything,
I am always praying for your happiness.
I'll never forget the nights you'd jet from the office
to pick me up from afterschool,
and head straight to *Medgar* for your night classes,
all without help.
You taught me that our goals in life
are attainable if we
remain persistent,
and that,
if we want to achieve something,
there is no giving up.
I'm very proud of you!
Rosewater to make peace with any storm.
Rosewater for tranquility.
Rosewater as a reward.
Rosewater for a new beginning.
Hard-work and persistence
has always been her blueprint.
I've never known a blessing to be tardy,
rather they are always prompt.
May you be blessed mom,
and that you also
find the rosewater that is hiding
in the many corners of this life.
What will I tell her when she calls me tonight
for a random chat about jokes and such?
I will tell her that I have conquered adversity,

and that more than ever,
my dreams are within my reach.
I will say that I am still writing and painting
because I have accepted art as my life work.
Hopefully this will make her proud of me.
Rosewater.

Rosewater for my aunty.
She will be home from work a little after dawn.
She will already have polished her home
and cooked a delicious meal.
Her joy would be found in watering her flowers
and speaking love onto them.
I will send her rosewater
to let her know that I haven't forgotten her.
I will send her rosewater
as an ingredient to add to her renowned wedding cakes.

For my friends,
when they are deciphering through emotions
and need an ear,
I will listen.
I will use rosewater to prepare drink.
Rosewater and lemon juice.
Sugar to taste.
Water to dilute, so that it's smooth enough
to quench the palette.
Dear friend,
today may seem like a mountain,
but tomorrow will be the beach.
It gets better.

For anyone healing or hurting,
I will make you rosewater.
It'll never run out.
There will always be enough,
and **you will always be enough**.
See you soon.

We will walk and talk,
and heal,
and eat,
and rest in the shade,
and be happy.

**I've made rosewater.**
**I'm making rosewater.**
**I will make rosewater.**

Rosewater is of roses and of water.
Rosewater is of labor and of love.

Sip drink,
and bathe,
from the crown of your head,
to the soles of your feet.
Begin anew,
blossom,
and be green.

Written with love
♥

www.ingramcontent.com/pod-product-compliance
Lightning Source LLC
Chambersburg PA
CBHW061730020426
42331CB00006B/1178